GRAND CANYON ARIZONA & NEW MEXICO

A PICTURE BOOK TO REMEMBER HER BY

Designed and Produced by
Ted Smart & David Gibbon

Featuring the photography of
Edmund Nägele F. R. P. S.

CRESCENT BOOKS
NEW YORK

INTRODUCTION

Arizona, as a classic symbol of America's Old West, naturally boasts an abundance of legends of the Indian leaders, Geronimo and Cochise, and of towns such as Tucson, where the feud between the Earp and Clanton brothers eventually erupted into the West's most famous shoot-out, the gunfight at the O.K. Corral. Characters and events such as these do not, however, belong solely to the world of fiction and films, for this, the 48th state to enter the Union does indeed boast a long and colourful history. Archaeological studies have revealed evidence of human settlement in the area from about 25000 BC and the dry sands of the desert have preserved cliff-dwellings, artifacts and even bodies belonging to the very earliest civilisations such as those of the Anazazi and Hohokam, and to successive Indian cultures. It was not until 1539 that the first Caucasian is known to have visited the state. Fray Marcos, a Franciscan, came to Arizona from Mexico to search for the fabled cities of Cibola and in the early days of Spanish exploration these legendary seven golden cities drew a number of die-hards to the Southwest but perhaps the first successful Spanish work is really attributable to the Jesuit priest, Eusebio Francisco Kino. Founding missions throughout Arizona and northern Sonora, in Mexico, he converted thousands of Indians and taught them agriculture and science. Yet for some considerable time the fierce Apache Indians prevented many from settling in Arizona. Furthermore the uprisings of 1802 and 1827 and the upheavals engendered during the Mexican Revolution forced the abandonment of all settlements, ranches and mines except those of Tucson and Tubac and in 1821 Mexico's flag replaced the banner of Spain. It was not until after the Mexican War that Arizona was ceded to the United States as part of New Mexico. Because of the gold rush in neighbouring California, Arizona's development was rapid and in 1912 it was admitted to the Union.

The Arizona of the 1970s with its modern cities, sprawling suburban developments and nationwide transportation arteries presents quite a different face. Large areas of desert have been transformed by colossal irrigation schemes into flourishing farmlands and ever-expanding cities, which like Phoenix, stand firmly rooted in the 20th century. Yet in its broad expanses of sparsely settled country and its spectacularly coloured rock walls rising above dramatic desert plains, in its mud adobe structures and baroque Spanish missions, Arizona has preserved much of the natural landscape that was so strongly associated with its frontier days. The state's awesome natural scenery has changed relatively little. Eerie ghost towns still huddle among primeval petrified forests, snow-capped mountains, dramatic gorges and rugged canyons.

Most breathtaking of all these natural features however, must surely be the Colorado Plateau, the world's most intricate and complex system of canyons, gorges and ravines, of which the trunk gorge, carved by the Colorado River is the spectacular Grand Canyon. This, the deepest and most impressive of all the Colorado Plateau canyons, frequently known as the "awesome abyss", is approximately 5,300 feet deep. Winding its way for 217 miles from the head of Marble Gorge, near the northern boundary of Arizona, to Grand Wash Cliffs, near the Nevada line, the intricately sculptured chasm of the Grand Canyon contains between its outer walls a multitude of other imposing peaks, buttes and canyons. Here too, in the exposed rocks of the canyon walls lies a unique time-scale of earth history for no other place displays such an extensive and profound record of earth events for analysis, dating and study. In general however, those who come to the Grand Canyon are drawn above all by the grandeur and the beauty of its rock strata...for the overall red colour of the canyon is delicately shaded with layers of buff and grey, soft green and pink and in its depths, brown, slate-grey and violet.

Visitors to New Mexico may be drawn by the same combination of rugged natural beauty and ancient historical interest. Historically New Mexico shares with Arizona much of its early Indian culture and subsequent Spanish colonisation. New Mexico was occupied by various Indian peoples for at least 10,000 years before the arrival of the first white explorers. As in Arizona it was reports of the Cities of Gold which brought the first Spanish adventurers to the area in 1540 and in 1595 contracts for colonisation were given to Juan de Oñate who made the first permanent settlements and founded Santa Fe in 1610. For some time missionary work predominated until in 1680 the Indians rebelled, driving many of the settlers away but by 1700 Spanish arms had reasserted themselves. New settlers arrived when the Santa Fe Trail was opened and in 1822 New Mexico became a province of Mexico until General Stephen Kearny occupied Santa Fe in 1846 and declared the territory part of the U.S.A. Two years later it was formally ceded to the U.S. but it was not until 1912 that it became the 47th State of the Union.

Today New Mexico still bears witness to its eventful history. Its capital, Santa Fe, the old southwestern terminus of the Santa Fe Trail, is the oldest continuously used seat of government in North America and in the vast flatness of New Mexico's plains and the rough weather-beaten peaks of its mountain ranges the state has retained much of the atmosphere of the frontier days of cattle drives, cowboys and clashes with Apache Indians. In the cities the influence of New Mexico's Indian and Spanish heritages and the Anglo impact on the two is everywhere apparent...in the arts in general but in particular in a unique architectural style based on Indian pueblo buildings modified in Spanish mission style. In the villages Indians perpetuate the traditions and skills of a bygone era in crafts such as pottery or blanket making and in the performance of native dances at innumerable fiestas. The most famous of these displays, the Inter-Tribal Ceremonial now draws thousands of visitors to Gallup every summer. Performances such as these take place against an ideal backcloth for like Arizona, New Mexico possesses an abundance of dramatic scenery. This is a state of eloquent natural contrasts: of the vast flat expanses of an extension of the Great Plains with the rugged heights of the Rocky Mountains and of dense pine forests, verdant meadows and fish-filled streams with arid wastes in which even cacti seem to struggle to survive. It is then appropriately, against scenery such as this and against apparently timeless landscapes shaped by volcanic formations and strangely eroded rocks, that the people of New Mexico have so successfully preserved their colourful heritage.

One of the world's most awe-inspiring natural features is the Grand Canyon *these pages and overleaf,* where two thousand million years of earth building lies exposed in the stratified rock that lines this most spectacular of the 19 gorges along the Colorado River. Seen from Pima Point *above,* the Colorado snakes along the floor of the majestic canyon.

The South Rim of the Grand Canyon affords a series of incomparable views. From two of the observation points along West Rim Drive, Hopi Point *above, left* and *overleaf* and Mohave Point *above and below right* and *below,* spectacular rock formations provide an unforgettable panorama particularly in the soft light of a setting sun or in the dramatic shadow of summer storm clouds.

In the course of some 6 million years the Colorado River, seen *centre right* from Lipan Point, has cut 5,000 feet down into the rock and differences in the relative resistance to erosion of the succeeding layers of stone have given the walls of the South Rim the rough steplike form clearly visible *left* from Moran Point, *above* from Yaki Point, *below right and overleaf* from Mather Point and *below* from Mohave Point. Mules *above right* provide the ideal means of transport along narrow winding cliff paths.

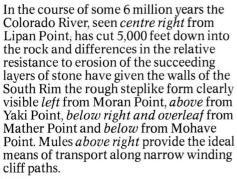

Begun in the autumn of 1971, the
construction of the village of Tlaquepaque
on these pages was the realisation of the
dream of Abe Miller, a Nevada
businessman who was inspired to build an
arts and crafts village in Sedona, Arizona.
In a setting of spectacular natural beauty
he created charming shops, galleries and
restaurants mainly in the style of Spanish
Colonial architecture decorated with red
roof tiles, flower pots, bells, statuary and
wrought iron work imported from Mexico.

Just south of Sedona, the huge and
colourful sentinels of 'Cathedral Rock'
overleaf form one of the most striking
landmarks of Oak Creek Canyon.

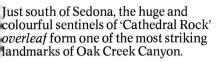

Oak Creek Canyon *above* and *above and below right,* is one of a series of steep-walled canyons dissecting the southern margin of the Colorado Plateau.
The sun sets *left* over the San Francisco Peaks rising from the 7,000-foot plateau near Flagstaff to a 12,670-foot tip. This, Arizona's highest point, has been a sacred mountain to Indians since the first memory of man in this region.
Melting snow crusts the White River at McNary *below.*

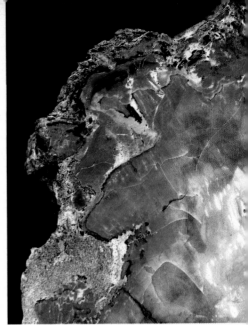

The Petrified Forest National Park in
northern Arizona is a fantasy landscape of
curious shapes and colours. Here in the
strangely eroded badlands viewed *above
left* from Blue Mesa, thousands of
petrified logs *above and below* lie
scattered, brilliant with jasper and agate.
Among the state's most fascinating
geological features are the Flattops *centre
left*, massive remnants of a once
continuous layer of durable sandstone
protecting a series of layered deposits that
have elsewhere been removed by erosion,
and the Tepees *below left*, small peaks
resembling tepees or haystacks showing
erosion of soft, layered clay deposits.
The Painted Desert *below right* was so
named by Spanish explorers because of
the brilliant colours of its waterless
plateaus, buttes and mesas.
Built in the 12th and 13th centuries
Montezuma castle *right* is among the best
preserved structures of its type. The
foundation is in a vertical cliff 46 feet
above the talus slope and it contains the
ruins of a prehistoric cliff dwelling.

The varying bands of colour representing the different rock types can be clearly traced through the cone-shaped hills of Blue Mesa *left*. All these formations are the product of erosion which continues to affect even the fallen logs. These will be gradually worn away to become tiny fragments like the pebbles on the trail. Lee's Ferry *above*, named after one of Utah's great pioneers, marks the point at which the mighty Colorado River issues from shadow into brief sunlight before plunging again into chasms of its own carving. Historically this interlude between the cliffs gave access from plateau to river and so made Lee's Ferry a corridor between Utah and Arizona. In the Marble Canyon *right*, sheer cliffs rise 800 feet on either side of the Colorado, spanned by the Navajo Bridge and *overleaf* in the Navajo Tribal Park, West Mitten, East Mitten and Merrick Butte rise imperiously from the floor of Monument Valley.

In the several thousand square miles that constitute Monument Valley, isolated monoliths of red sandstone tower as much as 1,000 feet above the sandy wasteland *above left, above, above right and overleaf,* and among these gargantuan rocks Indians still make their traditional homes *below.*

Five periods of Indian culture, dating from AD 348 to AD 1300 can be seen in the Canyon de Chelly National Monument *below right.* Among its principal remaining ruins is the White House *left,* which was actually occupied from 1060 to 1275 and which still nestles beneath the overhanging walls of a mammoth rock structure. From the floor of the same canyon, Spider Rock *below left* points its long, slender spire skywards.

The southern and western regions of
Arizona are desertlike but the striking
growth of desert plants includes a wide
variety of cacti. The desert in bloom is one
of nature's greatest miracles and among
otherwise barren wastes the exotic cactus
flowers bring life and vigour to an already
dramatic landscape.
above left: Grizzly Bear Prickly Pear
centre left: Hedgehog Cactus
below left: Organ Pipe Cactus
above: Totem Pole Cactus
right and below: Giant Saguaro Cactus

The 726-feet high Hoover Dam *above* is one of the highest dams ever constructed and impounds one of the largest artificial lakes in the Western Hemisphere whilst Glen Canyon Dam *left,* the fourth highest in the United States, impounds the 186-mile-long Lake Potwell as part of the Colorado River Project, so providing hydro-electric power for cities and industries throughout the West. London Bridge *above right,* which once spanned the River Thames in England, now crosses a manmade channel of the Colorado River in the Arizona desert. Transported block by block from London and reassembled in its original form, the bridge is a striking landmark in a planned international resort complex, which continues its English theme with a traditional 'pub' and telephone box *centre right* and an imitation Beefeater *below right.*

The Tonto National Monument *right and left* preserves the most accessible of south-central Arizona's prehistoric cliff dwellings, the remains of a two-storey adobe and rock house or pueblo, constructed in a natural cave.
East of Phoenix *above* a rainbow extends its multicoloured arch over Theodore Roosevelt Lake and in Tortilla Flat *below* a dummy suspended from a tree recalls the hanging of a convicted thief.
East of Mesa at the Gateway to the Valley of the Sun, Superstition Mountains *overleaf* silently guard the secret of the fabulous 'Lost Dutchman Mine'.

Phoenix viewed *above right* from 4th Avenue and Jefferson is the vital and sophisticated capital of Arizona and the industrial and cultural centre of the new Southwest. A number of fascinating works of art reflect the city's cultural interests. Outside St Mary's Church *above* Jerome Kirk's 'Phoenix Bird Ascending' rises from a sparkling pool.

One of John Vaddell's works, 'The Family' *below right* ornaments the central Court Building.

The State Capitol *centre right* is built of Tufa stone from Kirkland Junction and granite from the Salt River Mountains. Tempe, the Arizona State University *left* includes on its campus one of the last major buildings designed by Frank Lloyd Wright.

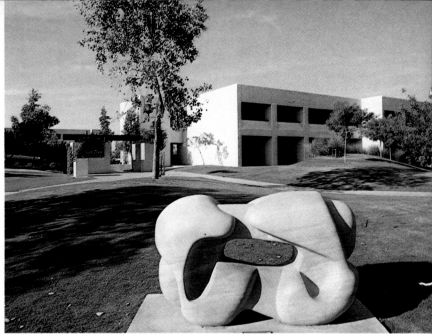

Tombstone *above and below left*, the 'Town too tough to die' was perhaps the most famous of America's old mining camps. Ed Schieffelin, the celebrated prospecter came to Fort Huachuca with a party of soldiers who, when he left them to prospect, told him that he would find only his tombstone and so when in 1877 he made some rich strikes, he named his first claim Tombstone.

The mountains of the Seguaro National Monument *above and overleaf* with their thickets of prickly pear and seguaro cacti, found only in southern Arizona and the State of Sonora, typify the Sonoran arboreal desert. Surrounded by the Paradise Valley resort area, Scottsdale is particularly renowned for its arts and crafts and for its civic centre which houses the municipal buildings, among them the City Hall *below*. On its Mall stands the celebrated statue of 'Freedom' by Robert Winslow *above right*.

Built in approximately 1350 by the Hohokam Indians, used for about a century and then abandoned, the Casa Grande *centre right* was discovered in 1694 by Father Eusebio Francisco Kino and today its ruins provide a fascinating illustration of the early Indian construction methods.

18 miles north of Nogales stands the abandoned Mission San Jose de Tumacacori. The massive adobe church *below right* was begun by the Franciscans in about 1800 and unfortunately never completed.

One of the oldest Spanish settlements in the West, Tucson *above*, with its imposing Pima County Court House *above right* and *below* and its Civic Centre *left*, grew up on the site of the Indian village of Bac. Mission San Xavier del Bac, known as the 'White Dove of the Desert', is shown *right*, and *overleaf* Organ Pipe Cactus National Monument.

The Pueblo de Taos, with its carefully maintained church *above left*, and terraced communal dwellings *above* and *below left*, tells of a culture hundreds of years old. North of Taos a three span continuous truss bridge *right* crosses the spectacular Rio Grande, while in the town itself can be seen the Kit Carson House and Museum *centre left*. The solidly built church *below* stands in the Ranchos de Taos, and *overleaf* is shown Shiprock rising more than 1,700 feet above the surrounding desert.

The Fort Union National Monument *above left* has preserved the ruins of the historic fort which between 1851 and 1891 supplied many outlying posts and protected settlers and travellers on the nearby Santa Fe Trail, the famous trail depicted in a wall painting *below* on the occasion of the Fiesta of Santa Fe.

San Miguel *above right*, constructed of adobe walls which are five feet thick, is the oldest church in the U.S.A. and the church *above* which dates from 1867 is the oldest Protestant church in New Mexico. The high altar *below right* is that of El Santuario de Chimayo. Built in 1813-1816 this is one of the most beautifully decorated churches in the Southwest. All the paintings and carvings were done by local native craftsmen. The same blend of art, history and spirituality is to be found in the 18th century mission of Santuario de Guadalupe *centre left* which has been recently renovated.

The Pecos National Monument *below left* includes pueblo ruins and the crumbling walls of old Pecos Mission, erected by the Franciscans in 1700 over the ruins of a previous church.

The annual 'Intertribal Indian Ceremonial' at Gallup in New Mexico continues the traditions and the culture for which this area is particularly renowned.

The El Morro National Monument or
'Inscription Rock' *above left* has served as
a 200-foot-high landmark since pre-
Columbian days and carved into its soft
sandstone are ancient Indian petroglyphs.
A tree stands silhouetted against the sun's
rays in the Gila National Forest *below left*
and nestling in a cavity beneath the
overhanging rock *below* is one of the
prehistoric dwellings included among the
Gila Cliff Dwellings.

Just east of Grants stands the Santa Maria
Mission *centre left* and the church of San
Felipe de Neri *right,* which was built in the
1700s, still holds regular services in New
Mexico's largest city Albuquerque, seen
above by moonlight.

In 1945, in a remote area of the White Sands Missile Range near Alamogordo, the first manmade atomic explosion sent a huge multicoloured cloud surging to a height of 40,000 feet and marked man's transition to the atomic age. Today the International Space Hall of Fame *centre left* houses exhibits honouring 40 space pioneers from various nations.

Southwest of Alamogordo, the White Sands National Monument *above* contains snow-white expanses of gypsum sand. Gypsum which is washed by rain from the mountains to Lake Lucero, is evaporated by warm winds and deposited as minute particles in dunes that rise up to forty feet above the valley floor.

Faintly outlined against the Organ Mountains *below left* are the pale crosses of Las Cruces. San Miguel Church *below* in Socorro was erected in its present form in the 1620s but it is still regularly used today. Southwest of Carlsbad with its Eddy County Court House *above left* are the Carlsbad Caverns *above and below right* and *overleaf*, a series of enormous rooms that form one of the world's largest caves. Delicate plant-like growths, massive stalagmites, stalactites and pillars, many of which are tinted by iron and other minerals, have been formed in a limestone reef by a process begun some 3 to 5 million years ago.

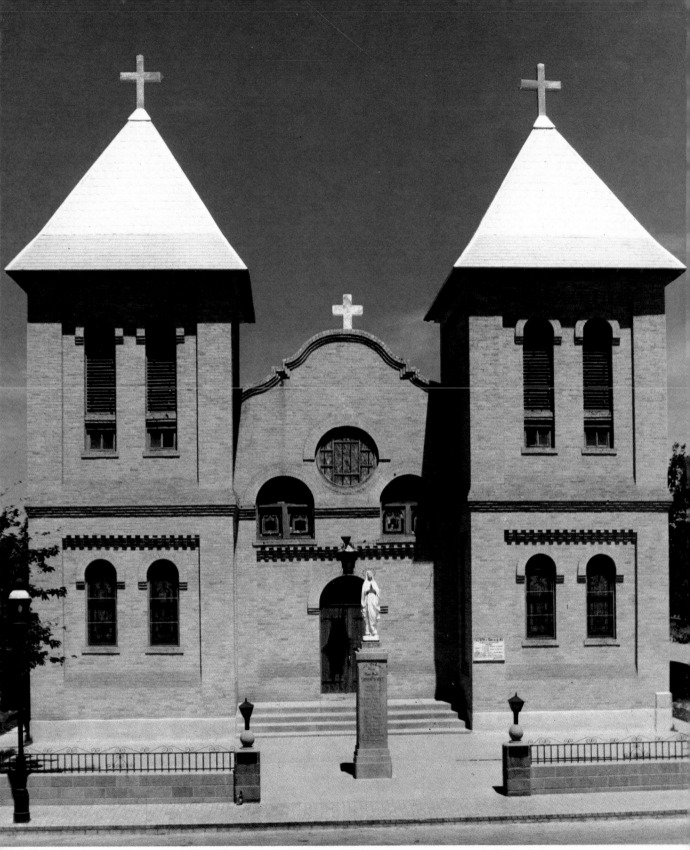

First published in Great Britain 1979 by Colour Library International Ltd.
Illustrations and text ©: Colour Library International Ltd, 163 East 64th Street, New York 10021.
Colour separations by La Cromolito, Milan, Italy.
Display and text filmsetting by Focus Photoset, London, England.
Printed and bound by SAGDOS - Brugherio (MI), Italy.
Published by Crescent Books, a division of Crown Publishers Inc.
Library of Congress Catalogue Card No. 79-51715
CRESCENT 1979